ILLUSTRATED BY CLAIRE CONWAY

SIXTY FOR 60

Simple Truths and Joys of Life

DANNY BADER

WITH JOEY BADER

© Copyright 2025 by Danny Bader. All Rights Reserved.

This book is protected by the copyright laws of the United States of America. No part of this publication may be reproduced in any format without prior written permission from the author.

Published by Desert Soul Publishing.

www.dannybader.com

Book cover design by Christy Day,
Constellation Book Services

ISBN (paperback): 978-1-7327066-1-3

Printed in the United States of America.

Preface

As I turned 60 and took a moment to reflect on my incredible journey through life, a few things came to mind-truths I've come to understand and simple joys that have brightened my days. It started as a list, something I wanted to share with others, so I posted it on social media. Then, our middle son, Joey, suggested, "Dad, we should make this into a book." So, here it is.

Thanks to Joey for his encouragement and to the amazing illustrator, Claire, for bringing this vision to life with her talent and support. This book is for you to consider and enjoy, no matter your age. I encourage you to always explore and be curious and to forever live your truth--life is too fragile and short not to.

We are wishing you much faith and fulfillment.

Peace,
Danny

To my Family & Friends

Thank you for the laughter, love, support, craziness, and countless quiet moments that have revealed life's greatest truths and joys.

Your presence in my life has helped me see that these simple truths and joys are never small and that the most meaningful wisdom is often right in front of us.

This book, Sixty for 60, is for you - because so much of it is because of you.

Luv ya.
Danny
May 2025

1. Your relationship with God is your strongest foundation for life.

3. A journal & a cup of coffee in the morning.

7. Top-down Jeep rides.

10. Pay attention to the leaves changing in the fall.

11. Loving someone from a distance is a huge form of self-respect.

12. Fresh tracks of snow on a powder morning.

13. Mothers are powerful (don't f*ck with 'em).

14. Pizza... Especially in Italy.

16. Lead with love.

17. Moderation with food & drink.

18. There's a fine line between "here" & "there".

19. A job you truly enjoy.

21. You can never read too many inspirational quotes.

22. Spontaneous moments of passion with your partner.

23. Put your phone away.

24. Family vacations are the best.

25. Sunrises are a great way to begin your day.

26. Sunsets can be wonderful wherever you happen to be.

27. Guinness _does_ taste better at the factory in Dublin.

28. Michelangelo's Statue of David has an energy to it — David looks <u>alive</u>.

29. Say, "No" more, so you can say, "Yes" to what matters.

30. Seek support — and look to support others who need it.

31. Clean bed sheets that were hung on a line.

34. If given the opportunity... Spend time with a person with a terminal illness.

35. Surround yourself with _good_ people.

37. Have a morning thought or ritual to get your day off to a positive start.

39. Visit a new place at least once a year.

40. Swimming Naked.

41. Candlelight.

42. Evil must be confronted & eliminated.

43. Beach Cruisers are the best bikes.

44. Music heals.

45. Signs from a departed loved one.

47. Being with loved ones during the holidays.

48. You are not here to have life beat you...

    trust me... it's the other way around.

49. There is someone out there for you.

50. A hot dog from the grill is a good thing — raw onions make it gooder.

52. Handwritten Notes.

Thanks so much for inviting me to your party! It was a great time & the food was great. Your house is lovely. I look forward to our trip this summer. Love ya!
♥

54. Your to-do list will never be done.

55. Purge your clothes & give them away twice a year.

57. Holding a newborn baby.

58. Silent retreats are gratifying.

Now it's Your Turn

Sixty for 60 is a collection of sixty reflections on the simple joys, hard-earned truths, and small moments that shape a meaningful life. Now, it's your turn.

Reflect on what's shaped you: moments, lessons, memories, or dreams. Write them down - one by one. A phrase, a sentence, a story, a quote, or even just a word. Draw an image that represents each one.

There's no perfect way. Just be honest. Be you.

And if you feel called - share it. With your family, your friends, your future self. Because sometimes a reminder of life's simplest joys and truths are the ones the world needs the most. Let your "sixty" keep you focused on what really matters...and keep them coming...

1. _____

2. _____

3. _____

4. _____

5. _____

About The Author

Danny Bader is an inspirational speaker and survivor of a life-altering electrocution accident that left him momentarily dead—before he came back to life. His powerful journey has inspired him to write five other books, including Back to Life: The Path of Resilience, Abraham's Diner, I Met Jesus for a Miller Lite, Taking the Sh*t Out of the Show, and A Radical Reverence for YOUR Life. A devoted husband and father of three, Danny splits his time between Conshohocken, PA, and Cape May, NJ, when he's not traveling to share his story and inspire others.

About The Illustrator

Claire Conway is a high school art and psychology teacher who loves to doodle. She also works as a commission based artist that creates illustrations and designs for weddings, birthdays, home decor, as well as any and all special occasions.

Check out some of her work!

Contact info:
Email: ClaireConwayArt@Gmail.com
Website: ClaireConwayArt.com

Social Media:
Instagram: @TheDailyDoodle.CC
TikTok: @ClaireConwayArt

www.ingramcontent.com/pod-product-compliance
Lightning Source LLC
LaVergne TN
LVHW061315060426
835507LV00019B/2169